I0139800

SHAKESPEARE'S "KING PHYCUS"

An Historical-Pastoral-Tragical Comedy in Five Acts

Tom Willmorth

BROADWAY PLAY PUBLISHING INC
224 E 62nd St, NY NY 10065-8201
212 772-8334 fax: 212 772-8358
BroadwayPlayPubl.com

First printing: September 2011
Second printing: December 2012
I S B N: 978-0-88145-493-2

Book design: Marie Donovan
Page make-up: Adobe Indesign
Typeface: Palatino
Printed and bound in the U S A

SHAKESPEARE'S "KING PHYCUS" was first
presented by The Strange Tree Group (Artistic
Director, Emily Schwartz) and The Lord Chamberlain's
Men (Producer, Ira Amyx) on 18 June 2010 at The
Building Stage in Chicago, Illinois. The cast and
creative contributors were:

PLAYER ONE...Michael T. Downey
PLAYER TWO .... Bob Kruse
PLAYER THREE ....Carolyn Klein
PLAYER FOUR .... Scott Cupper
PLAYER FIVE.. Delia Baseman
PLAYER SIX .... Stuart Ritter

Director ....Ira Amyx
Scenic designer...Jay Neander
Costume designer.. Delia Baseman
Lighting designer/Production manager.................Julian Pike
Original music .... Elizabeth Bagby
Assistant director/Dramaturg .... Emmy Kreilkamp
Production stage manager ....Rebekah T Johnson

CHARACTERS & SETTING

The play is intended to be performed by a cast of six (4 males and 2 females). Other casting configurations are certainly possible.

PLAYER 1 *(male)*, KING PHYCUS / CAESAR / SAMPSON / PETER / SANDWICH

PLAYER 2 *(male)*, GLOUCESTER / BRUTUS/ GOLDENBERG / ATHOL

PLAYER 3 *(female)*, MACBETTY / GERTRUDE / NURSE/ LEVUS / ROSENSTEEN

PLAYER 4 *(male)*, FRIAR DON / CHORUS / POTPAN / SARDONICUS / WALES / GRAVEDIGGER

PLAYER 5 *(female)*, JULIET / SOOTHSAYER / WITCH / GREGOLA / CLOWN / SOLDIER #2 / LAD

PLAYER 6 *(male)*, HAMLET / ROMEO/ EXTRANIUS

The action unfolds in numerous locations, including the streets of London and Rome, a haunted parapet, a Scottish heath, Bosworth Field, a friar's chamber, a bedroom balcony, and several rooms around PHYCUS's castle. As in other Shakespeare works, the establishing of locations should be done quickly, with minimal props and furnishings.

INTERMISSION

Although KING PHYCUS is a 5-act play, Shakespeare himself includes a halfway intermission point. It follows the CHORUS's speech at the end of ACT III, Scene 2.

PRELUDE SONG

(Sung to a tune suggestive of Greensleeves.*)*

Attend you lords and ladies all
Our grievous tale of wrath and wrong:
Tonight, Misfortunes on Phycus fall;
We pray your indulgence, 'tis two hours long.

Permit enactment of blood and pain,
Shun sympathy that bars us.
Should murder and madness thee entertain—
Perchance you'll enjoy a catharsis!

Hie, Hee, the Muses Three,
We pray inspiration shall strike us;
Hey Nonny Nay, begins our play,
The tragical tale of King Phycus.

The Pastoral-Comical, Lyric-Historical,
Tragical tale of King Phycus!

PROLOGUE

CHORUS:
O! for a Benefactor to assume
The daunting debt's expense of this production:
The funding for a stage, paycheques to act,
And coin enough to costume kings and queens!
O, then should fierce King Phycus and his foes
Be played by major stars, who on these boards,
Larger than life, 'ld die death on tragic death
For your enjoyment! —But pardon, patron friends,
Our flaccid fancy which doth dare attempt
To conjure for your eyes a Muse of fire!
And after plunking down thy ducats dear,
A Muse of steaming turd is all that's proffered;
Gentles, pardon. But, what didst thou expect!
For can this ebon-box hold England's realm?[†]
How should we shoe-horn in all ancient Rome?
Bethought you six poor players—mostly hacks—
Could populate a five-act history?
Well, pardon us! O pardon, pardon! ...Wait:
If thou wilt be complicit to this farce,
And willfully suspend thy disbelief,
Your sharp imaginations may ferment
The cheesy imperfections of our show.
Think, when we mention horses that you feel them,

---

† *Quarto 1 substitutes "grass bowl" for "ebon-box", suggesting an altered version to allow for indoor performances.*

Rearing mud-caked hooves upside your heads;
When one poor pimply walk-on with a stick
Declares himself an army, think it so;
Permitting the mathematics of your minds
To subdivide each extra to a million.
Shouldst thou recognize an actor in two roles
Do not inform thy neighbors, "Wasn't he
The soldier who was slain i'the second act?"
But turn a blind mind's-eye to double-casting.
For tis your thinking-caps must crown our kings,
Armour our guards, adorn our battlements.
An if you do, our humble acting crew
Shall dazzle thee with Phycus' story now!
This bargain twixt us made, we beg you stay,
Happily to hear, blindly to judge, our play!

ACT ONE

Scene 1

(A London marketplace)

(Enter SAMPSON *and* GREGOLA, *two English servants, toting shopping baskets.)*

SAMPSON: 'Ods my life, we shall not carry fruit!

GREGOLA: Nay, not a pip, for then we should be grocers!

SAMPSON: An we be grosser, Gregola, we'd reek.

GREGOLA: Then by the gross, I'ld buy thy reeky wit,
And wholesale mark you up.

SAMPSON: My wit's cashiered.
But I shall squeeze that grocer's tangerines
For selling us this wormy produce here!

GREGOLA: Content you, Cuz, and regulate thy spleen;
The marketplace is hot, and humoured thus,
We shall not 'scape a brawl. So let us leave.

SAMPSON:
Tis lettuce leaves that rot doth make me stew!
Our English peddle-carts enloaded be
With mealy rot; our finest fruits and vedge,
The pride of English farmers here at home,
Is shipp'd away by treaty off to Rome!
Our plummest fruit; the cream of all our wheat!
I'll sugar-beat the Roman next I meet!

GREGOLA: I beg thee, Sampson, come in from the street
Our good King Phycus hath proclaimed a writ
Arresting men for outbursts such as these.

SAMPSON: Behold this brick-like bread!

GREGOLA: Soft, pinch thy loaf!
For by my crusty heels here cometh two
O'the house of Romulus.

SAMPSON:To ream us, if they dare.

(BRUTUS *and* EXTRANIUS *enter, the latter toting a basket.)*

BRUTUS: Come, come, Extranius, bear my fruit before.

EXTRANIUS: So shall I, Brutus.

BRUTUS: Pah! I ate a fly!
These stalls must be where salads go to die.

EXTRANIUS:
The pickings here are slim; at home an ornge
Would be as large as Agamemnon's thigh
In full-out flex.

GREGOLA: Good Sampson, hold thee back!

SAMPSON: I'll bite my thumb at them, a gnarly taunt
To any he that bears it.
(He bites his thumb.)

BRUTUS: Do you bite your thumb at us, sir?

SAMPSON:
I do but bite my thumb, sir. Do you quarrel, sir?

BRUTUS: Quarrel, sir?

SAMPSON: Aye, sir!

BRUTUS: Maybe. Extranius, have we diplomatic
immunity if I say aye?

EXTRANIUS: No.

BRUTUS: No, we do not quarrel, sir.

SAMPSON: Then I but bite my thumb.

GREGOLA: As like do I.
A happy hangnail here I chew upon!

EXTRANIUS: Hey!

SAMPSON: Ho!

BRUTUS: Fie!

GREGOLA: Fa!

BRUTUS: Fing!
(He flicks his chin in Italian taunt.)

GREGOLA: Do you flick your chin at us, sir?

BRUTUS: Who, sir? Me, sir?

GREGOLA: You, sir!

BRUTUS: No, sir!

EXTRANIUS: We do but flick our chins. Fing!

SAMPSON: Draw, Gregola, an we be men.

GREGOLA:
And bear the wrath of Phycus full? Forefend!

BRUTUS: Do you quarrel, sirs?

SAMPSON: Nay, sir.

BRUTUS: No, sir? Well.
Spoken like a scurvy English dog,
And toothless, too.

GREGOLA: We art rubber; thou art glue.
What thou in wretched anger speakst, from off
Our spongy frames extern doth bounce away
And on thy pitchy backs doth fast adhere
To thus proclaim thy ignomy. So there.

EXTRANIUS:
Thy wordy sticks and stones hurt not our bones.
Thou art but swine.

SAMPSON: I know thou art, but what am I?

BRUTUS: Phycus fecals.

SAMPSON: I know thou art, but what am I?

GREGOLA: Sampson, hold thy peace!

BRUTUS: Nay, hold my piece, as did your mamma do!

SAMPSON: 'Spancakes! Have at you now!

GREGOLA: Turn, wops, and draw!

BRUTUS: By Jove, I'll wop thee strait!

(With bread loaves and fruit they fight. FRIAR DON enters.)

FRIAR: Peace! Peace! Will no one hear? Put up thy fruit!
By Jesu, I insist you cease your hate
And toss your bloody baguettes to the ground
And mark the wrath of this perturbéd priest!

(They drop their weapons.)

FRIAR: I'faith, I seminaried in the East
Where Shoalin Buddhists train'd me in their arts,
And If thou choose to cross me, by the rood,
I'll execute some Kung-fu on your ass!
These civil brawls, twixt you Italian types
And you disgruntl'ed hayseeds local-born,
Endanger every ardent peace accord
Old Phycus and thy Caesar hath enforced
To end the coffer-quenching costs of war.
Distemper'd hawks will kill a fragile dove.
Embrace as brothers, then, in Christian love,
That we together may, in holy swells,
Go slaughter Turks and other infidels.

SAMPSON: With charity we turn our other cheeks,
To offer but the wind that tween them sneaks! Pppth!†

(SAMPSON and GREGOLA exit gaseously.)

---

† *The first known example in English literature of an onomatopoetic oral raspberry.*

EXTRANIUS: Well, that's mature—I swear they're worse than Greeks!

BRUTUS: Thou, holy man of cloth—

FRIAR: 'Tis hemp.

BRUTUS: Whate'er—
You'll not compel my silence with thy prayer.

EXTRANIUS: A thousand thousand treaties cannot quell
Con brio Brutus!

BRUTUS: Know my title well,
For I am he shall give thy Phycus hell!
But first, let's share a bath at our hotel.

(BRUTUS *and* EXTRANIUS *exit.*)

FRIAR: O England all, to Jesu genuflect!
Evil omens, presagers of death,
Have late on country lane and copse been seen:
Horses eat each other; owls at noon
Make mockish hoot; odd comets blaze the night;
My rutabagas do not grow this year,
Despite my mindful tending. All such signs
Forbode ill days, ill deeds, ill-bred designs.
Board up thy windows, then! Stock cannéd good!
O England, pray for Phycus and his brood!

Scene 2

(KING PHYCUS's *throne room*)

(*Fanfare. Enter* PHYCUS, HAMLET, *his wife* MACBETTY,
JULIET, GLOUCESTER *the hunchback, and* POTPAN, *a
servant. All kneel before* PHYCUS, GLOUCESTER *with great
effort.*)

PHYCUS:
Attend to Brutus, embassy of Rome...Gloucester.

GLOUCESTER: Ah!
(He hobbles up and exits.)

PHYCUS:
Whilst Richard makes like bunny down the hall
We now express our featur'd purposes.
Give me the map there, ho!

POTPAN: *(To* MACBETTY*)* He call'd thee "ho!"

MACBETTY:
Bestow the map, slave! Here, my gracious lord.

PHYCUS: Lo, eighty years of bloody strife is done;
Green England is at peace with prickly Rome,
And since my royal legacy's assured—
And old queen Gertrude's dead and buriéd—
It is my fast intent to steppeth down,
And, shuffling off my saggy mortal coils,
Crawl toward death—or nail a trophy wife!
Upon this—Where's the map!

MACBETTY: Your lordship.

PHYCUS: Zounds!
Know then: our kingdom's lands are divvied up
And likewise split in twain's our present power.
Where be my spawn, my two beloved kids?
Stand forth, Prince Hamlet! And, yea, his Scottish wife
The Thaness Cawdor, dame Macbetty!

MACBETTY: Sire.

PHYCUS: And stand forth, too, our treasured Juliet!

JULIET: In sooth, methinks my little heart will break
To see my father age.

PHYCUS: What sayst thou?

JULIET: Nothing.

PHYCUS: Nothing?

JULIET: Nothing.

PHYCUS: Nothing? O. Methunkst I heard you speak.
My lords, this hour we publicize our wish
To fast confer the powers of my rein
Upon our legal heirs; my scepter, seal,
And this damn'd heavy crown I do exchange
For silver hair and golden parachute.
Tell me, children, who doth love us most?
The choicest woods and beachfront properties
I give whoe'er the loudest toots my horn.

JULIET: No horny flattery can Juliet make.
What can I say but love and honesty.

PHYCUS: What, Juliet?

JULIET: Nothing.

PHYCUS: I saw thy mouth just move—else I be mad?
Hamlet won the coin toss, speak thee first.
What sayeth Hamlet, rightful son and heir?

HAMLET: A little more than air, but less than heir!

PHYCUS:
Thy quip, no doubt, works better seen in print.

HAMLET: In five-fold blazon publish my despair.

PHYCUS: Is't possible you're melancholy still?

HAMLET: My mother, sir, did die within the hour.

PHYCUS: Thy mother, Hamlet, died a year ago.

HAMLET:
She's two months dead! Nay not so much, not two!

PHYCUS: Hours, months; the gorgon's in a box!

Her bucket's kick'd, however long it seems!

HAMLET:
"Seems" my lord? Nay, "is"! I know not "seems"!
My seems is "is"; if is is is in this. Is. O!

MACBETTY:
Permit me speak, for Hamlet's passive voice
Belies the active nature of his soul.

PHYCUS: Our Hamlet's wife, Macbetty, has the floor.
Don't Scotsman-like be thrifty with thy praise.

MACBETTY:
Thy son and I do love you more than words,
Than fame or fortune, lands or liberty;
Than jewels, kittens, warm-knit satin sashes,
Snowflakes that stay upon nose and eyelashes,
Than brown papyrus parcels loop'd with string,
Than prancing Austro-kinder, nuns that sing,
We love you this much!

PHYCUS: For thy rich reward—
All lands, from this crease here t'the goblet ring,
Including Bernam Wood and all this tan,
We make thee lord and lady! Come, come, my quill!
(He marks the map.)

MACBETTY: Husband Hamlet, damn it, be a man!
You sulk in silence whilst I brown my nose!

HAMLET: Methinks I hear my mother.

(GLOUCESTER reenters.)

GLOUCESTER: Good my liege,
The embassy of Rome is here at hand;
The brutish Brutus clambers fitfully
To pour some bile in thy ancient ear.

PHYCUS: O, Gloucester, let him cool. His Latin rant
Shall keep the gate until my daughter speaks.

JULIET: O, I am sick, and feel my acid flux.

PHYCUS:
Come, Lord Gloucester; goodman Richard, come,
And heed my praise from lovely Juliet.

JULIET: As happy as I am, I cannot heave
My heart unto my mouth in flattery.
You have begot me, bred me, loved me, father;
Saw to my health, my tutoring of arts;
Thou mortgaged Greenland to the Swedish hordes
That thou couldst pay my orthodontic care;
And my intrinsic innocence declares
I love you all, with duty's recompense,
No more nor less.

PHYCUS: What part of half the map did you not get?
Thy feeble compliments embarrass me,
And I upon this gerrymandered map
Did set aside for you the amplest parts.
But let that slide. Thou getst another chance:
This noble Duke of Gloucester, Richard called,
I have bequeath'd your hand in marriáge.
Thy wedding day is set for Thursday next;
Once wed these lands become your bridal gift.

GLOUCESTER:
I would I might have woo'ed thee on a date;
But as I stand, few women think me straight.
You'll learn to love me, lady, I've a hunch.

JULIET: To lose my virtue here, I lose my lunch!
I cannot heave my heart into my mouth,
And yet methinks I heave— Whoo, whoo, whoo!

GLOUCESTER: My gorge doth rise to hear it!
(*He exits.*)

MACBETTY: Mine doth too!

ALL: Whoo, whoo, whoo.

HAMLET: Thy dry-retch, sister, doth infect the room!
Keep thy stomach, else we all shall spewm!

MACBETTY: Dispatch the girl!

POTPAN: Come, Juliet, away!
Nigel, Nimrod, fetch some sawdust here!

JULIET: Good father, pardon me!

(JULIET *and* POTPAN *exit.*)

POTPAN: And watch the rugs!

PHYCUS: This fickle ipecackic episode
Dissuades me not; her hand shant be denied!
A' Thursday Gloucester weds this bulimic bride!

(BRUTUS *enters.*)

BRUTUS: Phycus, turn you now! I shall not wait!

PHYCUS: O, Brutus, there you are; wherefore so late?

BRUTUS: Thy citizens have mock'd me in the mart
With rustic rudeness unforgivable.
All treaties I rescind, and leave for Rome.
But know, by Jove, that Brutus vows revenge:
I'll plead in Caesar's ear—the one that works—
To march against thy shores, and I shall see
Soft England lick the boot of Italy!

PHYCUS: (*Kicking* BRUTUS)
Why, here's thy boot! And here's thy boot again!
A butt-kick battle I can't choose but win!
Where be my guards!

BRUTUS: They exeunt severally!†

(*Exeunt* BRUTUS *and* PHYCUS *severally. Enter* FRIAR, *hurried.*)

FRIAR: Good Hamlet, bless thee!

HAMLET: Go'gi'go'den, Friar Don.

FRIAR: O prince, besnap thee from thy morose mood,
For I have wonders strange I must report:
Methinks I saw your mother!

HAMLET: Mother! When?

---

† [Q1] *Likely a stage direction wrongly assigned to*
BRUTUS.

FRIAR: Last night by chance I brought the Eucharist
To sanctify the night-watch in the tower;
Twas there we saw her eerie phantom form,
I swear before we'd even touch'd the wine.

HAMLET:
Great Gertrude's ghost! Perchance she'll walk again?

FRIAR: At midnight's bell she takes her spectral stroll.
This very night thou mayst encounter her.
Deus ex machina, boy, and quick apace!

HAMLET: Mother, I come! Friar, take me to this place.

(HAMLET *and* FRIAR *exit.*)

GLOUCESTER: MacBetty.

MACBETTY: Richard.

GLOUCESTER: So. It twould appear
That you and I alone do keep our heads.

MACBETTY:
My head, howe'er, doth wear an offered crown
Whilst thy affections Juliet rebukes;
To view thy freakish frame the princess pukes!

GLOUCESTER: Albeet at birth I was not fairly stamped,
My charms at wooing women are undamped.

MACBETTY: Ha! I damp myself to think it!

GLOUCESTER: She'll relent.

MACBETTY:
Thou vile, skew-stance, freakish malamorph,
Who can't withal ascend the stairs of power
Without assistive ramps—wilt thou be king?

GLOUCESTER:
Now by this hand, an' this orthopedic shoe,
My body once was good enough for you.
Recall the winter we did castle up
At Inverness?

MACBETTY: Thou wert a stepping stump
To greater opportunes, and nothing more.

GLOUCESTER: To Hamlet mean you?

MACBETTY: Mean I England's throne.

GLOUCESTER: Deserves Macbetty better. When you bed
Thy mamma-minded melancholic prince,
You doubtless think on me from time to time.

MACBETTY: Twas heathen, harsh, unholy—

GLOUCESTER: Yet—

MACBETTY: Sublime.

GLOUCESTER: Then couple with me now in this design:
Old Phycus is a vegetable, who's roots
Are stump'd at garden-variety politics.
When grafted firm in marriage to his saps,
We'll foul the fruit with pesticidal tricks
And reap the windfall both.

MACBETTY: I'll tote that bucket;
If treason be in season, we should pluck it.
If thou should wield the scepter, I the orb,
The world will cry out—something that rhymes with
   orb!
Come, thou evil hunchback'd Machiavel!

GLOUCESTER:
And you, the grossest she-beast, black as hell.

MACBETTY: You do go on. But let's conspire then;
When in-laws turn outlaws; —they rule i'the end!

(*Exuent* MACBETTY *and* GLOUCESTER.)

END OF ACT ONE

ACT TWO

Scene 1

(CAESAR's palace in Rome)

(Enter SARDONICUS and SOOTHSAYER severally.)

SARDONICUS: O, citizens of Rome: Glad Lupercal!
High Caesar thanks thee much—now back to work.

SOOTHSAYER:
Beware Sardonicus! Fear the Ides of March!

SARDONICUS: Avaunt thee, prophetess! No time have I
To hear thy ravings.

SOOTHSAYER: I speak naught but sooth.
Let me see the palmside of thy hand.

SARDONICUS: I'll show thee palmside, hag. Now back
thee off.

(BRUTUS enters.)

BRUTUS: Rome!!

SARDONICUS:
But Mars be praised, I here detect a friend.
Hail, Brutus!

BRUTUS: Hail to thee, Sardonicus!
Come, let me grip thy forearm manfully!

(A mighty cry of "Caesar" off.)

BRUTUS: What shout is this so unified of pitch,
That though it be a crowd ten thousand strong
It soundeth like twas voiced by three or four?

SARDONICUS: Know you not the cause?

BRUTUS: I've new arriv'd
From Phycus fretful court this very hour.
Our legions might betopple Phycus now
With Caesar's sovereign say-so.

SARDONICUS: Save thy breath:
His temperament hath alter'd since you left.
High Caesar hears the vox of populi
Who, lib'rate now from eighty years of war,
Collective cry, "Great Caesar brings us peace;
Let's lick his feet in thanks!" and on this day
Do elevate his status to a god!"
But here comes Caesar now.

(*Enter* CAESAR *and* LEVUS, *and with them* ROMEO *dressed in Italianate doublet, jerkin, and hose.*)

CAESAR: I thank thee, yea!
I thank thee all! Calm down!
Levus, take my robes. They stainéd are
With grubby handprints of this faithful throng.
And if this ragu can't be lifted forth
Do make a note the laundress to behead.

LEVUS: Her name is prick'd in wax.

CAESAR:
Then come, good Levus, strip my garments off;
And ev'ry loyal Roman, strip thee too,
That all a-buff we'll share a public bath,
As did we do in Caesar's salad days.

BRUTUS: Hold the dressing! Lord, first Brutus must
Expose some naked truth.
(*To* LEVUS)
Leave us. Leave us.

(Confused, LEVUS *moves away.)*

CAESAR: My dear friend Brutus, new return'd to Rome:
O, let me grip thy forearm manfully!
Sardonicus, I greet thee with a nod.

SARDONICUS:
Thy chin-wag is too much; I give thee thanks.

BRUTUS: Great Caesar, I from England's chalky shores
Have travel'd swift to impart pressing news:
That frail King Phycus hath—

CAESAR: Excuseth me.
You yammer, Brutus, in our useless lobe
And all I hear is tinny echoings.

ROMEO: Ay, me!

CAESAR: But who is this that sighs?

ROMEO: Forgive me Caesar. As befits my youth,
My idle mind did recollect a maid,
Who dwells within my heart a forsook love.

CAESAR: I know thee not. Who book'd my entourage?

ROMEO: My name, high Caesar, Romeo is called;
A delegate from fair Verona, where—

CAESAR:
What wear'st thou, boy? These funky fashions clash
With Roman togs.

ROMEO: These are the latest weeds.
A stylish renaissance sweeps cross your land;
Calf-enhancing pumpkin pants and hose
Preferréd are through all of Italy.

CAESAR: We shun such fads; although it would be nice
To not side-saddle ride on battlefields.

BRUTUS: To battle, Caesar! Yea, my very theme.

CAESAR: fla-Fla, fla-Fla, fla-Fla; that's all I get!
Just stand in line, good Brutus, on my right;

To thee I'll ope my operative ear
But first must hear petitions from my plebes.
(*To* LEVUS)
Levus!

(LEVUS *starts to go.*)

CAESAR: Levus!

(LEVUS *returns.*)

SARDONICUS: Brutus, Romeo, speak with me apart.

CAESAR: Read the petitions!

LEVUS: The owner of the Circus Maximus,
Declares he shall to Sparta relocate
Unless the city builds at its expense
A Colloseum new and state of art.

CAESAR: And so we shall. Increase the gaming fee
And tax all merchants deeper by a groat.

LEVUS: I prick it so. The next petitioner,
Requests that we invent the letter U,
That V is overused, and oft confused
With numeral five. And here is signed "Thy friend."

CAESAR: Ah, yes. Our good Ugina. Prick it so.
The next petition read!

(*A* SOOTHSAYER *emerges from the crowd on* CAESAR's *left.*)

SOOTHSAYER: Beware the Ides of March!

CAESAR: Who calleth from the crowd so cryptically?

SOOTHSAYER: I am a soothsayer, Caesar, say I sooth!

CAESAR: Is this some tongue-twist riddle test of tooth?

SOOTHSAYER: Beware the Ides of March!

CAESAR: Behold my thighs are large? Can this be truth?
Suggest you that my gluteus expands?

BRUTUS: She is a dreamer, Caesar. Let her pass.

SOOTHSAYER: Beware thy senate, Caesar!

CAESAR: I fear thee, wench!
Leave us!

(LEVUS *goes to* CAESAR.)

LEVUS: Lord?

CAESAR: What?

LEVUS: Methought—!

CAESAR: Alack, my brain!
White fuzzy spots mine eyne doth entertain!
(*He falls.*)

BRUTUS: Caesar falls! Levus!—

(LEVUS *begins to depart.*)

BRUTUS: Levus!

(LEVUS *returns to* BRUTUS.)

BRUTUS: Take him, sirrah, and young Romeo;
Lead him from the public haunt of men
Lest rumors spread of his infirmities.

(ROMEO *and* LEVUS *exit carrying* CAESAR.)

SARDONICUS: The emperor is sick!

BRUTUS: He tired looked
And somewhat jitteréd.

SARDONICUS: Like Pompeii he shook!
Brutus, I respect how fond thou art,
And know you tender Caesar as thy friend,
But one frail man shan't power dominate
As Caesar doth! Let's act e'er it's too late!

(*An off-stage shout*)

SARDONICUS:
Hark! The citizens renew their lusty cheers.

BRUTUS: Young Romeo returns! What news of Caesar?

ROMEO: We witness'd here a royal epilepse.
O, never saw I such a spectacle

As Caesar's seizure.
Caesar's seizure.
Caesar's seizure.
(After some attempts, he achieves the phrase.)

BRUTUS: What was the second shout?

ROMEO: When Caesar rose to orate once again,
The emperor was struck—O, bless the day!—
A narcoleptic napping episode!
In very mid-thought snapp'd he to a snooze
And smacked the pavéd stones.

SARDONICUS: The family curse.
His lineage by now is so in-bred
That shallow flows the jinxt genetic pool:
Epilepsy, narcolepsy, yea,
Wherever there's a lepsy leaps he in!
And this they call a god! He must not lead!
An earthly intervention Rome doth need!

BRUTUS: I fear thy mind!

ROMEO: I too.

CROWD: *(Rhythmically chants, off)* Caesar, Caesar!

ROMEO: But list, they chant again!

SARDONICUS: We must persuasive oratory make
Like Pompey past, with Rome itself at stake!

(The rhythmic chant of "Caesar, Caesar!" continues for a time as the triumvirate speaks to the crowd.)†

SARDONICUS:
Tax for the aqueducts, tax for the archways!

---

† *It appears this oration sequence was popular enough with 16th Century audiences that it transferred to English pubs and music halls. Although not attributed to Shakespeare, his speak/sing styrle was later used by American composer Meredith Willson in the* Rock Island *number of his Broadway hit,* The Music Man

BRUTUS: Tax for the Pantheon, tax for the porticoes!

ROMEO: Tax for the Forum, tax for the statuary!

SARDONICUS: Tax for the famous roads and viaducts
   and cobblestoning!

BRUTUS: Tax for the atria and stadia and sewer system!

ROMEO:
Friends, lendyer ears, lendyer ears, Fellow Romans!

BRUTUS: Thou can praise, thou can praise,
Thou can pribble, thou can praise,
Thou can praise, praise, praise, praise Caesar all you
   want
But he's weaker than he was.

SARDONICUS: And he knoweth not the territory!

ALL: Nay, sir! Nay sir!

ROMEO: Why, he preens like a peacock as he's prickin'
   a petition
For a fellow politician like a flim-flam, grease-palm!
God's wounds! Aye, sir!
And all the while he looketh like a relic
In an outta date toga.

BRUTUS & SARDONICUS:
Whattya talk, whattya talk, whattya talk, whattya talk?

BRUTUS:
And the people he impresses when he goes like a god
In the market on the Lupercal. E'en so,
Caesar swooned, and he fell, and he foamed,
And he frets-frets-frets-frets-frets.

ROMEO: Sayest what!

SARDONICUS: He is no god!

ALL: Nay, sir! Nay, sir!

SARDONICUS: He's a Mortal Man!

ROMEO: He's a what?

BRUTUS: He's a what?

SARDONICUS:
He's a mortal man, with a tendency to totter
And to sacrifice our honor and give it away
To a king like Phycus!

ROMEO: Peruse the panorama and enumerate the hills:

ALL: (Counting) Hill, hill, hill, hill, hill, hill— Hill!

ROMEO:
Seven hallow'd hills that enring around our Rome
And define our democracy.

ALL: Amen. *Et tu!*

BRUTUS: But a Caesar who's ambitious
Supersedes our civic wishes
So we must kill him now, to assert our aristocracy.

SARDONICUS: Ever know a ruler it was right to kill?

ALL: Kill? Kill? Kill? Kill? Kill? Kill?

SARDONICUS: Kill!

ROMEO: But we do it for the honor
Not the interest of our persons,
But the good of Rome.

ALL: (Slowing) O, yea! O, yea! O, yea!

BRUTUS: Now let's go and get our territory!

SARDONICUS: Brutus, come; let's carp the diem straight!
(He exits.)

BRUTUS: Romeo,
Request I must another task of thee:
When tyrant Caesar's dead, then Rome is free
To wend our mighty army England's way.
But hie thee thither first to glut your eye
With Phycus' castle secrets as our spy.

ROMEO: I go! Tho' sadly leave true love behind.
(He exits.)

SOOTHSAYER:
Beware the Ides of March, what did I say?
Can I in sooth prognosticate or nay?

BRUTUS: Be gone, thou blabbing hagseed!

SOOTHSAYER: Beware thee, Brutus, saturated fats
And German hookers—Fie, I've said too much.

(She exits.)

BRUTUS: What mean you, wench? I prithee, tarry! Wait!

(BRUTUS exits after SOOTHSAYER.)

Scene 2

(A battlement on Castle Phycus.)

(A bell tolls. PETER enters as a night watchman.)

PETER: Tis midnight now, and this the very stretch
Of castle wall where late that ghost was seen!
'Sdrats that I, who drew the trimmest straw,
Must wind up watch. Who's there, in Phycus' name?

(HAMLET hurries on.)

HAMLET: A friend!

PETER: Unfold thyself!

HAMLET: I Hamlet am.
The friar told me nightly here is seen
A ghostly visitor.

PETER: Aye, Lord, the queen.

HAMLET: My mother's spirit saw you with thine eyes?

PETER: Her every feature, prince, we recogniz'd;
She wore her beaver out.

(HAMLET strikes PETER.)

PETER: Her beaver coat, my lord! Her coat!

HAMLET: Forgive the muff.

(*Eerie music plays.*)

PETER: Alack, the ghost returns!

HAMLET: Dear God, the smell!
The air bereeks the sulfurous stench of hell!

PETER: I think that's me; by terror I'm unmann'd.
Come away, good Hamlet, come away!

(PETER *exits, ginger-quick.*)

HAMLET: Courage, pucker now, for I shall stay!

(*The ghost of* QUEEN GERTRUDE *enters, royally accoutered.*)

GERTRUDE: Hamlet! Hamlet, mark me!

HAMLET: O, my soul!
Art thou an angel bless'd, or fiend of hell?

GERTRUDE: I am thy mother.

HAMLET:
That doesn't narrow down the question much.

GERTRUDE: I am thy mother's spirit.
Doom'd to walk the night until my sins
From off my earthly flesh are burnt away.
Ill-fortunate, I died in formal wear,
So forced I am to haunt in painful pumps!
Twould sere thine eyne to see my bunioned feet.
And don't let's get me started on the heat!

HAMLET: O, piteous ghost,
Why must thy preciousness in torment dwell?

GERTRUDE:
Why, let me think. Perchance— 'cause I'm in Hell!
Thy mother snuff'd without a priest or prayer,
Condemn'd etern with limp, gray-rooted hair!
O, list you, Hamlet, list. I shall be brief:
I from the great beyond enlist thy aid,

To seek revenge upon the villain's life,
Who terminated mine in foulest murder!

HAMLET: Murder!

GERTRUDE: Murder most foul! Twas rumour'd out
That I was sleeping in the orchard grove
When chanced it I was by a serpent stung,
And quickly died. S'luck! What be the odds?
In truth, by poison I was quick dispatch'd:
An unseen perpetrator by me crept
And poured a mortal unction in my ear!

HAMLET:
Thy ear! O, heavens! —Flow'd the liquid through?
Wouldn't the drum—no matter. Mother, who?

GERTRUDE: Suspect I this, and in my soul tis true:
Thy father, Hamlet. Phycus filch'd my life.
In mid-life madness, wish'd he for a wife
With firmer flanks, and jugs symmetrical;
And nightly he corrupts our royal bed
With gold-dig bimbo blonds with air of head.
If ever Hamlet did his mother love,
Revenge my soul.

HAMLET: By all the Fates above,
A son cannot his mother disobey!

GERTRUDE: Then swear it Hamlet! Swear!

HAMLET: I swear, I swear!
For cat will mew, and double-dog will dare.

GERTRUDE: The threads of fate unravel; thou shalt be
The knot that ties them up: Remember me!
(She disappears.)

HAMLET: I shall remember, mother! And with resolve
I spring to action! And yet methinks again.
To be the knot, or not to be the knot. Or not.
What was the question?
To be this phantom's foil in this plot,

I risk a ride in Hades hand-basket.
Perchance some Fiend adopted mother's form,
And trolls the night in drag to tempt my soul;
Belike the queen's a queen; I am much vex'd
To be cross-purpos'd by a Fiend cross-dressed.
Yet, chance it were my mother; what of that?
My father's matricide must be revenged.
I'll... No!—no wait—Ah, yes!—Forbear —O, shit.
My thread of active thought becomes unknit.
To knot his noose, or snap her apron string?
Cook Father's goose, or grief to Mother bring?
O I'm a slave and roguish peasant thing
To contemplate my course, and kill a king!
(He exits.)

Scene 3

(JULIET's chamber)

(JULIET enters followed by POTPAN.)

JULIET: Alack, my life! On Thursday must I wed
The monstrous Gloucester. Would that I were dead!

POTPAN: O, wish it not, good mistress. Dry thy tears.

JULIET: O, Potpan, pity me! I am a maid
Soon made in bed and thus a maid unmade.
Such beds are graves, and I do live afraid
That soon in bed or grave I'm getting laid.

POTPAN: A maid unmade, yet maiden! Tis the way
A randy Catholic girl equivocates
Before a priest, and hymen redefines!

JULIET: O, where is my barfing bucket?

POTPAN: Neath the bed.
Thy father comes, and most perturberéd.

(PHYCUS enters.)

JULIET: Go'gi'go'deen, dear father.

PHYCUS: *(To* POTPAN*)* Slave, depart.
I'll have some private chat with Juliet.

*(*POTPAN *sadly goes.)*

PHYCUS:
I have remembered me, you'll hear our council.

*(*POTPAN *gladly returns.)*

PHYCUS: No, I was right the first time, get you gone.

(Exit POTPAN.*)*

PHYCUS: Now, Juliet, my every waking hour
Has been to see thee matched before I croak.
The Duke of Gloucester is a noted man.

JULIET: Lord, marriage is a gift I dream not of.

PHYCUS: What hinders you in giving up your love?

JULIET: Good father, I'm but thirteen years of age.

PHYCUS: Thy mother at thy years had birth'd two kids,
Gain'd sixty pounds, had varicoséd veins—

JULIET: The wifely duty frightens me, M'lord.
I read the pamphlet Friar gaveth me,
But youthful blushing overtook my cheeks.
From the oriental woodcuts in the back
I could decipher neither hind nor hair.

PHYCUS: Odds bodkins, child! Still, you get the gist.
And to this contract, girl, I shall insist.
I know thou art mature enough to wed,
At least sixteen.

JULIET: I'm thirteen. Ask the nurse.

PHYCUS:
That gossip's still employed? I needs must curse.
But if she can dispense the argument,
I'll call her forth. What, Nurse! What, Cockney Cow!
Make haste!

(NURSE *enters.*)

NURSE: Now by me brit'le bones and swollen feet,
The master calls—and when 'e calls I come.

PHYCUS: Quick tell me, Nurse, how old's my Juliet?

NURSE:
Now, by me troth, I've known the girl from birth
For I did nurse the whelpling at my dug,
And yea, can tell her age unto an hour.

PHYCUS: Be she sixteen?

NURSE: Lord, lord, an by my teef,
Tho' at me last exam I 'ad but four,
I'll wager two of my remaining chomps
That of all the days o'the year, on Lammas Eve
Shall Juliet be fourteen; I recollect
My daughter Susan—criss the cross o' Christ—
She wert too good for me, and died in birth
Entangled in my cord— alack the day—
An Sire, you did offer up a sum
To make employ my vacant drippy doogs
And nurse your very own.

PHYCUS: So she is how old…?

NURSE: Upon my wimpled brain, I have it etched:
Twas Lammas-tide, me husband Nigel then
Berated me for taking too much time
To wean the girls and tend his nightly needs!
O, how he curs'd me aereolies out!

PHYCUS: Which means she's…?

NURSE: So I did take some wormwood to my dugs,
Oh I did have a set of dugs back then,
And I besmeared my milky nurples up
With wormwood, as I say, a tetchy drug,
To wean thy sweet-faced daughter, and as more,
To act as a depilatory too,
For I had hirsute hoo-haws, being Mediterrane,

And Jule, tasting, spat and made a face,
And off with Susan ran outdoors to play
And never else did come to me for suck.

PHYCUS:
You're sucking now, and milking my good time!
How old's my child!

JULIET: Didst thou just say I played with Susan, Nurse?

NURSE: Lordie lord, you did! Thou wert inseparable.

JULIET: You said she died in neonatal noose.

NURSE: But thou did love her so, my heart did break
To from your arms my little angel take.
You'd romp for hours, playing seek and hide—

PHYCUS:
When was she born, you baboon; make it clear!

NURSE: On Lammas Eve at night, tis fourteen years.
My ta-tas tingle still when I recall—

PHYCUS: Enough!
I get the Williams at the very thought.
The gist of all's she's old enough to wed.
Now, get thee gone! Vamoo, fat babbler.

(*Exit* NURSE.)

PHYCUS: Now list to me full well. My sole desire
Hath ever been to see thee wealthy wed.
Day, night, morn, noon, wake, sleep, pert, numb,
My brain did singly on thy welfare zone.
I make the choicest match, and what do you?
Thou spits me in the face! Implore no more!

JULIET: O, Father, hark me! Would that I were proud—

PHYCUS:
Father me no fathers, nor proud me no prouds!

JULIET: Wed me not, I beseech thee—

PHYCUS: Wed-me-not no wed-me-nots, nor beseech me
no beseeches!

JULIET: Aye, me! O, woe!

PHYCUS: Aye-me me no Aye-me me's; nor O-woe me
me no O mo me moes—!
Zounds!
Tomorrow will you wed!

JULIET: I must, I fear.

PHYCUS: Then here's thy bucket. (*Calling off*) Juliet
comes; stand clear!

(*Exuent* JULIET *and* PHYCUS.)

END OF ACT TWO

ACT THREE

Scene 1

(A Scottish heath)

(The distant drone of bagpipes. MACBETTY *and* GLOUCESTER *enter, carrying bags of golfing clubs.)*

MACBETTY:
Come, thou lame-legg'd, doddling duffer, come!
The sunlight wanes; we must attack the course
Lest falling dusk doth black beshroud the green.

GLOUCESTER: So foul a fairway have I never seen!
My golfing handicap I need not tell;
Tho clubb'd in hand, I'm clubb'd of foot as well.

MACBETTY: Then rest we on this rising ridge a spell.
Behold you, Richard: all these lands are mine.

GLOUCESTER: I'faith, my in-law'd sister, you receive
Those Birnham Woods; yon fens and leas I hold.

MACBETTY:
Those are the Glengarry leas; to you, they're gold:
And you don't get them; nay, not til the time
Thou art to Princess Juliet betroth'd.

GLOUCESTER:
The time's tonight, when Phycus fills his house
With gala guests to watch me wed my spouse.
When done, I'll chip the titleist from his halls,
And scorn the sandy trap in which he falls.

MACBETTY:
Tee up your courage! Now, I fear we've lost our balls.

(*A cackling* WITCH *enters, with boiling cauldron and ingredients.*)

GLOUCESTER: Alack, what hag hysterical is this?
Some vexéd spirit?

MACBETTY: Tis a Scottish witch:
They haunt the heaths and doglegs hereabouts.

WITCH: Boil, boil, charméd pot,
Throw in all this crap I brought:
Eye of earthworm, tongue of dog,
Wart of St. John—and of frog,
Lip of chicken, leg of snake,
Sliver'd mint of urinal cake.
Last in—the coven's secret scoop...
Condenséd cream o'mushroom soup.
For a fiendish spell of trouble
In the cauldron boil and bubble—

MACBETTY: Stay, craz'd cackler! if thou be of earth,
And know black-magic arts of prophesy,
Then ladle up the future destin'd me.

WITCH: Macbetty, Macbetty, Macbetty:
Thou shalt rule where Phycus stood
A tyrant all invincible,
'Mune from death til Birnam Wood
Doth march from off its hill.

MACBETTY: Invincible til pines themselves uproot?
Thy boding boldens me; I thank thee, Coot!

GLOUCESTER: In turn now presage me: I bid thee do't!

WITCH: Laugh at death, and rivals scorn;
Fear not mortal sword nor knife,
For never man of woman born
May harm thy charmed life!

GLOUCESTER: No man of woman born may kill me? Ha!
Unless there be some hidden metaphor—

(*A drum*)

WITCH: A drum, a drum, my master's come!
By the twitching of my nose,
Something wicked that way goes!
Bewitched! The charm's wound up!
(*She exits.*)

GLOUCESTER:
These drums announce the start of Phycus' feast;
The king's a lamb to slaughter, we the beast,
To fell him tooth and claw!

MACBETTY: I think it good,
Let's claim the crown as shark or tiger would!

(*Exuent* MACBETTY *and* GLOUCESTER.)

Scene 2

(*A hall at* PHYCUS' *castle*)

(*Enter* POTPAN *and* PETER, *scurrying.*)

POTPAN: Wag, servants, wag! Hie thee 'bout the house,
the guests are come! What, Buckler, Coalcart, Forkface;
where be these lads? Gravyboat! Jockeybox! Nimrod!
Sirrah, Peter, ho!

PETER: Aye, sir, Potpan! Aye, sir!

POTPAN:
Where be Sugarscrote, that he forgets the plates!

PETER: He clears this chamber, tables, rugs and all,
to host the evening's merry jigs and rare theatricals.

POTPAN: I beseech thee, Peter, are the musicians come?

PETER: Aye, sir, the musicians are here and tuned.

POTPAN:
The master will be pleased. Who plays tonight?

PETER:
Well, we hath Who on lute, Wherefore's on tabor, and I-Know-Not's on bass.

POTPAN: Sayst thou?

PETER: I say Who's on lute, Wherefore's a' tabor, and I-Know-Not's on bass.

POTPAN: Hired you a lute player?

PETER: Verily did I.

POTPAN: Then name the name of he on lute.

PETER: Who.

POTPAN: The lutist's name.

PETER: Who.

POTPAN: The lad on lute.

PETER: Who.

POTPAN: The loutist's name!

PETER: Who, I say. Who's on lute.

POTPAN:
That's what I asketh thee! Have thee a percussionist?

PETER: Aye.

POTPAN: His name?

PETER: Wherefore.

POTPAN: Because I wish to know the villain's name! Who's on tabor?

PETER: Nay, Wherefore's on tabor; Who's on lute.

POTPAN: I know not!

POTPAN & PETER: Plays bass!

POTPAN: Fool, get thee gone! I name thee Ass!
Give me men with honest English names;
What, Sugarscrote! Dillrod! Poopshoot! James!

(PETER *exits, as* HAMLET *enters.*)

HAMLET: Sirrah, are the actors come who play tonight?

POTPAN: Aye, m'lord. And here they come on cue.

(*Exit* POTPAN, *as* GOLDENBERG *and* ROSENSTEEN *enter.*)

GOLDENBERG & ROSENSTEEN: Our good lord Hamlet!

HAMLET: My friends from Wittenberg!
How dost thou, Goldenberg and Rosensteen?
What happy chance alights you at our court?

GOLDENBERG: Since flunking Wittenberg for lack of wit,
We travel 'round as hired players both.

ROSENSTEEN: Tis true; we're actors now!

HAMLET: Well lucky you!
What might have I in England seen thee do?

ROSENSTEEN: We play not England much.

GOLDENBERG: No, we grew tired
Of pigeon-holing roles and stereotypes.
Full oft were Rosensteen and I pre-cast
As minor friends who show up in Act Three
To play but foolish foils to the leads,
Then die off-stage in insignificance.
Eschew me roles like that!

HAMLET: Eschew I shall.

ROSENSTEEN: So moved we both to Italy and learn'd
Commedia dell 'arte improv skills.
And now we're back.

HAMLET: How does your act?

GOLDENBERG & ROSENSTEEN: It kills!

HAMLET: What script play you for Phycus?

GOLDENBERG: We use no scripts,
But ad lib stories that the crowd suggests.

HAMLET: If thou canst fashion fiction from a whim,
Suggest I this most sly scenario:
Tonight before the king you'll re-enact
The tragic telling of my mother's death;
Murder'd in the orchard as she slept
By potent poison poured into her ear!

GOLDENBERG: Poured in her ear? The poison?

ROSENSTEEN: Flows it through?

HAMLET: Don't asketh me; I heard it from a ghost!

(Offstage laughter)

HAMLET: Stand thee apart; Here comes the happy host.

(GOLDENBERG *and* ROSENSTEEN *move away*)

HAMLET: As they present the woeful act on-stage,
I'll watch my father's face, if he's awake;
If he but blench or arch his eyebrow so,
I'll know his guilt, and gut him on the spot!
Where lies my sharpen'd dirk?

(Exit HAMLET. *Enter* PHYCUS, JULIET, *and* POTPAN.*)*

PHYCUS: Gentle friends, I welcome one and all!
Come, ladies, doff thy shoes and cut the rugs;
Tonight we feast my daughter Juliet
Who takes in marriage Richard's wither'd hand.

JULIET: I wish to wed for love.

PHYCUS: Still she complains!
I'll smack thee to next fortnight for thy pains!
(He smacks her.)
 Drink, friends, drink! It is an open bar!
(Smack)
Go to, harlot! Slut-bag—Everybody dance!—
You'll wed for love! Go to, go to!
(Smack)

(JULIET *sulks away, and stands alone.*)

PHYCUS: Where's Macbetty? And my humped son?
He'll get a second hump ere this night's done!
Heh, heh. Come musicians, play!

(*Dance music plays, and dancers dance. Enter* ROMEO.)

ROMEO: This is the house of Phycus. Here must I
Serve Rome's intelligence as secret spy.
I'll quick peruse the room, and then depart,
That Brutus may his armies—Stay, my heart!
What angel, vision, goddess stands before
That all the other dancers fade from floor?
O she doth teach the torches how to glow,
And their back-lighting through her dress doth show.
I'll touch her hand, or I'm no Romeo.

(ROMEO *takes* JULIET's *hand; she wipes it on her dress.*)

ROMEO: If I profane with nervous sweaty hands
Thy precious palms, the reason I confess:
Twas thy attraction overworked my glands
And caused you wipe my moistness on your dress.

JULIET:
Good stranger, you do wring your hands too much;
Twas mine own clamminess I rubbed away.
Then place your hands upon my waist, like such,
That we might closer dance and sweatless stay.

(ROMEO *steps on* JULIET's *foot.*)

ROMEO: If I with damnéd klutzy, clod-like feet
Profane thy toes, this lame excuse I make:
When dancing I have trouble with the beat,
But to impress, bold steps I tried to fake.

JULIET: Thy soul is soft, however hard it lands.
I pray, good prancer, let's go back to hands.

ROMEO:
Have not saints hands, like ours that kiss in prayer.

JULIET:
Our hands are laymen; lay them down with care.

ROMEO: Let hands do like lips do; they explore...
(The lovers explore what hands do, in balletic hand-jyve.)

JULIET:
Say-say, O playmate: can lips like hands do more?

ROMEO:
Some lovers' handy tongues may wordless quote
In perfect verse.

JULIET: Be my vers'd kiss!

(ROMEO and JULIET kiss.)

JULIET: You kiss by the throat.

PHYCUS:
What man is this that gropes my child betrothed?

ROMEO: Is she the princess Juliet? O cursed fate!
My only love sprung from my only hate!
(He escapes.)

GOLDENBERG:
We know this man; we toured Verona once.
Tis Romeo, a youth of Italy.

JULIET: O, Romeo a Roman! Woe is me,
To swap salive with a mortal enemy!

PHYCUS: Thou foul, flirtatious flooz! Get to thy room,
Where for this night I make thee prisoner;
Tomorrow morn you'll seek the friar's grace,
Then off to chapel you'll be dragg'd apace,
And on my word, you'll suck on Gloucester's face!

(JULIET exits as HAMLET enters.)

PHYCUS: Here's merry meltdown. Gentles, revel on!

HAMLET: Thy railing, father, hath the party poop'd.
But I have remedy; let's watch a play!
A mirthful comedy, if all approve it.

ALL: Yea.

HAMLET: Then sit thee down, and give it up anon
For Goldenberg and Rosensteen! You're on.

GOLDENBERG: How doth everybody do tonight? Great!
To start we need a suggestion for a play;
A situation, prithee; shout it forth!

HAMLET: A royal queen
Who unsuspecting in her orchard sleeps.

GOLDENBERG: Alright, I heard: royal queen who
unsuspecting in her orchard sleeps. We act it now.
Curtain.

(In dumb show, GOLDENBERG *and* ROSENSTEEN *enact a
king wooing a lounging queen, picking pantomime fruit, etc.
Eventually,* POTPAN *and* CLOWN *reenter the scene.)*

PHYCUS: Hamlet, what sort of play is this?

HAMLET: A theater game, my lord.

PHYCUS: What call they it?

HAMLET: The Mousetrap.

PHYCUS: Now by Saint Agatha, it runneth long.

HAMLET: Shh! It is the argument of the play
Express'd in dumb show.

PHYCUS: Dumb indeed. I liked those singing cats.

HAMLET: *(Aside)*
Here comes the lurking killer by the queen;
My father's guilty visage to betray!

(A suspenseful moment)

ROSENSTEEN: Alright! At this point we need an object;
Something a lurking killer might use.

PHYCUS: A vile of mortal poison!

ROSENSTEEN: A vile of mortal poison.

HAMLET: Wormwood, wormwood!

ROSENSTEEN:
I heard vile of poison first. The lurking figure comes—

PHYCUS: No! A banana! I change my royal mind.

GOLDENBERG: A banana!

POTPAN: A rolling pin! Do that!

CLOWN: Nay, a colander; and put it on your head!

PHYCUS: I said banana! Do banana!

POTPAN: A wooden phallus!

OTHERS: Yes, a phallus! Use phallus!

HAMLET: Stop! Lights, lights! Give o'er the play!

PHYCUS:
That's it, the party's done! All go away! All go way!

(Exuent all but PHYCUS.*)*

PHYCUS: Next time they'll use banana when I say.
(To audience)
M'lords and ladies, 'trieve your cloaks and gloves
And hie thee home; the wedding is postponed.
Tomorrow it shall be, at break of dawn.
Til then, good night. Alack, fetch me a torch!
If thou brought boxéd gifts or cards or cash;
Just place them on yon table as you go.
Again, good friends, good night.

(Reenter GLOUCESTER, MACBETTY, POTPAN *and* CLOWN.*)*

GLOUCESTER: Phycus, spare a word ere you depart.

PHYCUS: Let's all to bed. We'll want an early start
Tomorrow when I wed thee to my child.
Go'gi'good'een, say I. Now humbly bow.

MACBETTY:
Contraire, old man. You'll bend before us now.

PHYCUS: Haggis eater! Bow, or lose my lands!

GLOUCESTER:
Thy lands are ours, bestow'd by Fate's commands.
Renounce!

MACBETTY: I wish no blood upon my hands.

PHYCUS: But my heirs—

MACBETTY: You stupid, ancient, catatonic fool!
Your children never shall in England rule.
Consider yourself usurped.

PHYCUS: I lose my mind!

GLOUCESTER:
Come, kitchen staff; this old buffoon to bind!

POTPAN: Forgive us, sire; our soft allegiance splits:
They offered workman's comp and benefits.

(MACBETTY *plucks* PHYCUS *by the beard.*)

PHYCUS: You pluck my silver beard! Insult me not!

MACBETTY: Did that insult you, sir? We'll I was taught
A worser insult back in grammer school:
A wedgie up the crack!

PHYCUS: Saint Melvin! No!
To thus betray my hospitality
And steal my throne? I'm cursed I did not see.

GLOUCESTER:
And blind, old man, thou'lt ever more shall be!

(GLOUCESTER *snatches a kitchen implement from* POTPAN
and extracts an eye from PHYCUS.)

GLOUCESTER: Out, vile jelly! Aye! Aye!
Out, ocular oleo! Mind's-eye marmalade!
Out, corneal compote!

MACBETTY:
Pluck out the other! That peeper pre-serve there!

GLOUCESTER: His other ball refuses to unlodge!

(One eye hangs dangling from its socket. MACBETTY *pries at the dangling eye, unsuccessfully.)*

MACBETTY:
Then let me do it. Out, visual viscous! Damn!
Just kill him, Richard! How I fear his look.

GLOUCESTER: I'll need a sharper implement than this!
(He exits.)

MACBETTY: Slay him, Richard! Ere he slink away!
My first decree with crown upon my head:
Kill Goldenberg and Rosensteen.

CLOWN & POTPAN: They're dead.

MACBETTY:
And fetch me lotions; this had best wash off.

(Exuent MACBETTY, POTPAN, *and* CLOWN. HAMLET *enters.)*

HAMLET: My father prostrate prays! I'll do it pat—
And with a laundered spirit bleached of sin
He flies anon to Heaven April fresh.
Which would be scanned, my Mother un-avenged.
So ope, cruel king, the windows of thy mind,
To see the verdict dealt by Justice—Blind!

(PHYCUS raises his face to HAMLET.)

HAMLET: Horror! Horror! It gives the heebee-geeves!

(HAMLET tries to stab PHYCUS, but is repelled by the heebee-geeves.)

PHYCUS: O, prithee, friend, I beg you take my life!

HAMLET: How pity now my spirit overtakes.
He's guilty, sure, but I will tweak my voice
And take an antic disposition on
And lead him safe away.
(In madcap voice)
Hey, hey, old codger! I'm foolish tho' I'm wise!

PHYCUS:
My fool? Yorick? I thought that you were dead!
Well, ain't you a sight for gored eyes!

HAMLET: Come, Nuncle, let thy Fool help thee flee.
The witless lead the blind in our family.

(HAMLET *leads* PHYCUS *off.*)

CHORUS: How swiftly 'pon thy thoughts our story flies;
Soon star-cross'd lovers, hunchback tyrants, ghosts,
Crazed kings and knaves and Romans on the rise
Shall clash in climax; which your Chorus boasts
Achieves cathartic clip—as each one dies!
But now, procure some wine thy thirst to slake,
Or sneak a smoke, or piss for comfort's sake
For Chorus here must intermission take.

END OF ACT THREE

(Intermission)

ACT FOUR

Scene 1

(Hall of PHYCUS' *castle)*

(A bell tolls. GLOUCESTER *enters. Shortly* PETER *enters, accoutered as a watchman, carrying a tapir.†)*

PETER: M' Lord?

GLOUCESTER: Who's there?

PETER: A watchman with a tapir, good m'lord.
Tis dark, for it is night; thy shadowed face
I can make barely out. Tis very dark.

GLOUCESTER: Tis nearly morn, so sirrah, get to bed.

PETER: I'll carry with me, though, this burning torch.
How dark it is!

GLOUCESTER: I've been informed. Good night.

*(*PETER *exits.)*

GLOUCESTER: The fairest Juliet at light's first glint
Shalt be enforced to bride it at my side.
For though I am not shaped for sportive tricks,
And ever wert at kick-ball chosen last,

---

† *A corrupted spelling of taper. Clearly, the servant is intended to carry a torch or lantern. Period accounts indicate that one production baffled the audience when the "tapir-bearer" entered carrying a small anteater-like ruminant.*

The princess shall assure my place with kings
When consummation coronation brings.
(MACBETTY *enters with* PETER.)

MACBETTY: Sirrah, hast thou seen the Duke?

PETER: Yonder, m'lady, murkily illumed,
For by my soul, it's really really dim.
(He exits.)

MACBETTY:
Richard, where's blind Phycus? Seek him out.

GLOUCESTER: I shall proceed no farther in this business.

MACBETTY:
We've scotched the snake, not killed it. Git 'er done.

GLOUCESTER:
Hast thou forgot the fortunes which the witch
In double dose bestowed upon our backs?
That thou would reign til Birnam Wood would march,
Whilst I to none of woman born could lose?

MACBETTY: Thou swore to kill the king, now be a man.
My fem'nine instincts teach me how t'would feel
To nurse a babe and give it mother's milk.
But had I sworn to kill, as you to this,
I would displuck my nipple from its gums
And dash it fiercely 'pon the jagged rocks!

GLOUCESTER:
Dash your nipple upon the rocks? Wherefore?

MACBETTY:
Would dash the baby's brains upon the rocks!

GLOUCESTER: Aye, yes, of course. But if we fail?

MACBETTY: We fail!
But screw your wicky to the sticky place
And we'll not fail.

GLOUCESTER: Thou hast my gall restored.

MACBETTY: Then find the king!

GLOUCESTER: Indeed, but ere I do:
I must beshave myself and shower take
And for my royal wedding ready make.

(*Exuent* GLOUCESTER *and* MACBETTY.)

Scene 2

(JULIET's balcony and a garden below.

(JULIET *enters above.*)

JULIET: Gallop in place, retarded be thy speed
You Phoeban ponies! Sink in muddy clouds,
And bring to crawl his westbound morn's commute
That day might never come. O day! Alas,
I must with Gloucester wed with nocturne's pass.

(*Enter* ROMEO *below.*)

ROMEO: What soft light breaks from yonder balcony?
Tis sure the east, where Juliet be the sun!
See how she leans herself upon that rail
In quiet contemplation of the stars?
Were I that shimmering star in Juliet's eyne;
O, what the hell; I would I were that rail.

JULIET:
O, Romeo, Romeo, why must Rome have Romeo?
Deny thy country; spurn thy title, yea,
For e'en thy name shows Rome shall end in naught.
Put O to Rome, and Romeo prevails.
What's in an O? This ciphered nil which yields
The sum of nothing, this zip, this egg of goose,
This hoop of nada, yea, this Fortune's Wheel,
Which should I spin, I'd like to buy a vowel,
And buy this O, and make of Rome a Romeo!

ROMEO: Shall I puzzle more, or shall I speak at this?

JULIET: O, cherished night, where is my Romeo!

ROMEO: My love!

JULIET: What man art thou that in the shrubbry creeps
Beneath my chamber, like some Tom-o-peeps?

ROMEO: I know not how to nominate myself.
My name, by thy account, amounts to none.

JULIET: What, Romeo! And Roman!

ROMEO: Yes, my love!

JULIET: I hoped, yet fervent feared, you'd safely fled.

ROMEO:
Thy orchard walls were high and slick with dew,
And have been here entrapped since yesternight.

JULIET: Romeo, if thou love me—

ROMEO: O, I do!

JULIET: I have a plan of Cupid's own device...

NURSE: (Off) What, Juliet!

JULIET: Oh, God, it is my Nurse.
Quick, secret thee within a shrubby cloak.

ROMEO: I shall secrete myself.

(NURSE enters.)

NURSE:
Gog's wounds, m'lady! Zounds, it breaks my heart
To see the castle fall to disarray.
Thy father blind, thy brother skipp'd the coop,
And rumors of a landed Roman horde.

JULIET: Alack, good Nurse, whatever shall I do?

NURSE: Beshrew my heart, but I methinks it best
That thou obey the Duke and wed with him.

JULIET: Peace, you traitress, go!

(NURSE exits.)

JULIET: Hsst, Romeo, hsst! O, that I did possess
A birding voice to lure him back again.

(JULIET *signals with a cooing birdcall.* ROMEO *responds
with a raven cry.*)

JULIET: My dove?

ROMEO: O, Juliet, I heard the grave report,
And fear these ill events shall thwart our love.

JULIET: If whirlwind marriage do content you, lord,
And offer you a faithful heart's accord,
I am thy wife.

ROMEO: I swear by Hector's sword—

JULIET: Swear not by that, some Roman battle thing,
But swear instead on Nature's offering.

ROMEO: Then by the Sun—

JULIET: Not that! I spurn his beams!

ROMEO: Then by the virgin moon—

JULIET: Not in thy dreams.

GLOUCESTER: (*Off*) Juliet! Thy husband calls!

JULIET: Alas,
Tis Gloucester, by his voice!

ROMEO: Into the shrub.

(ROMEO *disappears as* GLOUCESTER *enters.*)

GLOUCESTER:
Where is my bride? Where is my luscious—'Spants!
Why aren't thou dressed? It is our wedding day:
The guest are come, the caterer is paid,
The bridal bed with harness retrofit,
And still you're jammified.

JULIET: I could not sleep,
With sweet anticipation of the deed.

GLOUCESTER:
Well, sure. And I shall be thy morning dove.
Coo, coo.

(ROMEO's voice makes birdcalls from below.)

GLOUCESTER: What is that?

JULIET: Tis the lark, the herald of the morn.

GLOUCESTER: That's not a lark.

(GLOUCESTER calls as a bird. ROMEO's voice replies.)

JULIET: It is the nightingale
That nightly sings in yonder pomegranate tree.

(ROMEO's voice makes an assortment of bird calls.)

GLOUCESTER:
That's not a nightingale. And that's not a pomegranate.

(NURSE enters, screaming.)

NURSE:
Now, by my holidame, the prince is mad! Help! Help!
My Lord, I heard much cursing in the hall,
And saw twas Hamlet, madly disarrayed:
His shirt untucked, his doublet all a-muss;
His ebon tights about his feet, and jerkin off.
His jerkin jacket off. Methinks he's mad.
And lo, his worship comes.

(HAMLET enters, accoutered as foretold.)

JULIET: Oh, bless thee, brother.

HAMLET: Get thee to a nunnery!

JULIET: O, what a noble mind is here o'erthrown.

NURSE: Alack the day!

HAMLET: (To NURSE) Get thee from the balcony!
(To JULIET) Get thee to a nunnery!
(To GLOUCESTER) Get thee to a laborat'ry!

Because I'm mad!
Nuttier than Christmas fudge, I trow!

GLOUCESTER:
You'll summon cogency enough to answer this:
Where is thy father?

HAMLET: Father, let me see.
If a mad old dad, be a killer and a cad,
Where do you think he went?
With an eye for a lady,
And a look that is shady,
He's probably bound for Kent.
Via Saint Ives.
And while he was going to St. Ives,
He met a king who killed his wife,
With a distilléd poison.
Hoo, I'm being mad again!
Get me to a distillery!
(He exits, hopping over his downed pantaloons.)

GLOUCESTER: Sound the alarum, call the castle guard!
If he abet the king, it shall go hard.
I'll kill the prince, by poison, and/or by sword;
And Juliet, our marriage shall go fore'rd.

JULIET: Indeed it must, but ere we open gift,
I must to Friar Don for sacred shrift.

GLOUCESTER: Thou hast one hour; Nurse give me a lift!

(GLOUCESTER mounts the NURSE, who piggy backs him off.)

JULIET: Romeo?

ROMEO: *(Unseen)* I am here.

JULIET: Meet me anon at holy Friar's cell.
Once wedded there, our fortunes shall be well.

Scene 3

(A wilderness)

(Enter PHYCUS, *whose eyes are bandaged and bloody. One eye hangs some inches down by its cord.)*

PHYCUS: Yorick?

HAMLET: *(Unseen)* I am here!

*(*PHYCUS *lifts his eye to search.* HAMLET *enters.)*

HAMLET: Come, good Nuncle, take my helpful hand.
The morning wakes, and shakes her blondéd locks
Against the azure sky; the perfect hour
To take a sight-see tour away from court.

PHYCUS: Yorick, I am blind.

HAMLET: Hey nonny.

PHYCUS: Look!
They plucked one clean from out its orbit hole
And left the other dangling by its string.
Our face, once stamped for coins, is now a toy
For cruel Life to play at cup and ball.

HAMLET: I bandaged thee, good Nuncle, best I could,
And here have found for thee a forkéd stick,
To cradle up thy peeping pendulum,
That thou might take a glimpse at what's ahead.

PHYCUS: What lies ahead is ruin, wrath, and wrong;
The Three R's of the primer book of kings.
O leave me, Yorick, to my prayers and death.

HAMLET: Knock, knock!

PHYCUS: Who's there?

HAMLET: "Smellmyp."

PHYCUS: "Smellmyp who?"

HAMLET: Hey, nonny.

PHYCUS: Good one, Yorick. Now I do recall,
Why we did sell you to the Danish court.
But now with Death himself I'll have my sport!
Undiscovered country, here I come!

(PHYCUS *dashes off.*)

HAMLET: Nuncle, nay, run not with sticks. Thou'lt put
   thy eye out.
Nuncle! Father! Wait!

Scene 4

(FRIAR's *chamber*)

(*Enter* FRIAR *with* JULIET.)

FRIAR: Come, Juliet. And come forth, Romeo.

ROMEO: *(Unseen)* I am here. Alack, I'm there anon.

FRIAR: Now Romeo and Juliet, away!
I have in secret wed thee at thy hest,
But now in haste you must elope along
To live in...Mantua? I'll write thee there.

(ROMEO *enters.*)

ROMEO: Good Friar Don, a word: there yet remains
One last adventure here to be preformed.

FRIAR: Jesu, can'tst thou wait? Well, lustful be—
But make quick shrift; the last confessional's free.

ROMEO: Good parson, my intents are raunchless! No!
I need from thee a poison!

FRIAR: Poison!

ROMEO: Please!
In wedding Juliet, I have become
A prince of Phycus' royal family.
I'm duty-bound to lead his tatter'd troops
And 'gainst my former Roman comrades clash.

But knowing Brutus, were I capturéd
He'd torture from my brains our stratagems;
In such a case, a poison I'd ingest.

FRIAR: Such mortal drugs I have, but stand distress'd
To be the means of thy demisédment.
But here's thy deadly draft: don't take with food;
And be you Hercules, it will dispatch you straight.

ROMEO: God speed, fond pharmaceutical friar.
And, Juliet adieu! I must to war.
(He exits.)

JULIET: O, Friar comfort me!
Should I unto the castle now return,
The hunchback Gloucester takes me for his wife;
Ere make the two-back'd beast, I'd take my life!

FRIAR: If thou hast courage, girl, to off thyself,
I have a plan that may breed happy ends.
Take this potion, drink it ere you sleep:
And through thy veins will slink a seeming death;
Twill steal thy beating heart, and heat, and breath.
Tis likely Gloucester will not want you then.
Then—Romeo! He's gone. I'll send a note—
Thy husband, victory fresh, will ope thy crypt,
And wake you, take you, to Mantua you're shipp'd!

JULIET:
O poison is healthful, when for true love it's sipp'd!
(Enter GLOUCESTER.)

GLOUCESTER: Go'gi'goo'den, Friar Don. And Juliet,
Go'gi'goo'goo-goo. Giddly-Goo'gi'di'goo!

JULIET: Forgive me, Lord. I'm here for holy shrift,
And prayerful thoughts prevent a babe's response.

GLOUCESTER: Tis well you pray. Thy father was corrupt
And by report thou hadst one bad mother—

JULIET: Shut your mouth!

GLOUCESTER: I'm just talkin' bout shrift.

JULIET: I ready am to keep my father's bond,
And take you for my honor'd huoo.
Huoo. Huoo.
Excuse me, Lord.
(She exits a-heaving.)

GLOUCESTER:
Methinks it, Friar Don, some stealth's at hand.

FRIAR: None but the holy mysteries, good my Lord.

GLOUCESTER: Noted wide it is thou dost dispense
Of benedictions, baby sprinkles, yea;
But also unction, homegrown drug, and weed.

FRIAR: I dabble in the herbal arts, my Lord,
But only craft medicinal amounts.

GLOUCESTER:
I'll need from thee a deadly poisonous draught,
One drop of which upon a bladed sword,
Will poison him who suffers but a scratch.

FRIAR: I daren't supply the remedy you seek.

GLOUCESTER:
You frown, good friar; but what say my regime
Applied apothecaries such as thee
With stricter regulations of thy trade.
With paperwork thy monks we'd over-cram
You'd loath to brew a single blesséd dram.

FRIAR: *(Presenting a vial)* Here.

GLOUCESTER: *(Confidentially)* And have you…?

FRIAR: I'll skin a lamb.

(Exuent FRIAR and GLOUCESTER.)

Scene 5

(JULIET's *chamber*)

(JULIET *enters, a poison vial clutched in her hand.*)

JULIET: Good night! I'll tuck myself; again good night!
I have an icy portent in my veins;
What if this unguent doesn't work at all?
Shall Gloucester wed me then. Forbid it, no!
This dagger shall prevent it.
(*She shows a blade in her thigh garter.*)
Sit thee there.
What if this be a poison! Ponder that.
Belike the Friar turneth murderous
For what he thinks I know of legal suits
Allegéd by those former alter boys.
I think it not; he is a holy man.
But how if—here's a fearful point—how if
I waken in the crypt before the hour
That Romeo come to claim me. Holy shrift!
To slowly perish bolted in a tomb,
Where frisky risen ghouls seal thy doom,
As dancing deadmen romp in search of blood
To terrorize y'awl's neighborhood!
Holy Saint Michael, no! Romeo I come!
My husband and my lord, I drink to thee.

(JULIET *tries to drink, but as is her wont, begins to gag and spray.*[†] *Enter* FRIAR, NURSE, *and* PETER. FRIAR *brings flowers.*)

NURSE: Juliet, what slug-a-maid! What bed sore, Juliet!
I told thee, Friar. See, the child's up.

FRIAR: Jesu in a jumpsuit, what is this!
You were to drink the bottled sleeping draught.

---

† *Legend suggest that an early actor playing Juliet maintained a spit take riff for sixteen minutes.*

JULIET: I'm sorry, I regurgitated. Hic.

FRIAR: Dear child, thou art dazed but not be-dozed.
A moment and the spell will take effect.

JULIET: What, Friar, flowers!

PETER: The cleaning crew chipped in.

(JULIET *begins to hand out flowers in her stupor.*)

JULIET: This is a pansy, it's for remembrance.
This is rue, it is for homeliness.
This is rosemary, it's very good in fish and pot roasts;
These are poppies.

FRIAR: Poppies will make her sleep.

JULIET: These are for…
(*She falls aslumber.*)

FRIAR: Juliet! Alas no pulse or breath!
Now by the rood, good Juliet is dead!

NURSE: O, welladay!

PETER: We must inform the Duke.

FRIAR: Good Peter, do.

(*The sound of military trumpets.*)

PETER: What fearful tootle's this?

FRIAR: The Roman legion boasts with lungs of brass
It's eagerness to wend its warring mass
Gainst eensy England. Help me tote the lass.

(JULIET *is carried off.*)

END OF ACT FOUR

ACT FIVE

Scene 1

(Near Bosworth Field)

(Enter BRUTUS *and* EXTRANIUS.*)*

BRUTUS: Extranius, ascend this craggéd bluff
To better view the vast processional
Of fiery phalanx glitt'ring in the sun!
 Quake you, England; Rome is at thy gates!

EXTRANIUS: Lo, Brutus, Phycus' castle is in sight!
The troops await thy go-word's forceful flight
From out thy lips!

BRUTUS: Behold my mighty legions!

EXTRANIUS: I'm sure they are but cold sores, royal lord.

BRUTUS: Our Roman forces fill the landscape up!
How many men?

EXTRANIUS: A thousand score!

BRUTUS: What's that?
Look I like Archimedes? Do the math.

EXTRANIUS:
Full twenty thousand men are here amassed;
The puny English force is far outclassed.

BRUTUS: Extranius, go! Our western columns lead
To hunt the prey as master of our breed.

*(*EXTRANIUS *exits.)*

BRUTUS: *(To an audience of soldiers)*
Men of Rome, we'll battle on this day,
Like tameless mongrels; Yea, like dogs of war!
Unleash our canine constitutions, all!
Show snarling teeth, and sniff them in the rear!
Like demonic, smoke-enblastéd hounds of hell
We'll overleap their fences, charging hard,
And paw the frail petunias in their yard.
And grip their legs like labs in heightened heat
And uncontrolléd hump them saucily!
We'll enter their enforcéd castles in
And on the costly drap'ries lift our legs;
Upon their royal carpets shall we sit
And scoot our hyper heinies cross the floor
Til they are forced to shoo us out the door
And cry out, "Bad! Bad! Here slid the dogs of war!"
Come, soldiers, let's embark!
(He exits woofing.)

Scene 2

(Another part of Bosworth Field)

(Trumpets. Enter in the DUKE OF WALES, SOLDIER #2, *and* EARL OF SANDWICH *dressed for battle.)*

WALES: Brave lords, and earls and thanes of every clan,
Together must we forge a brother's band
And fight as one 'neath Romeo's command.
(To Soldier #2)
Who art thou, soldier? Hold, our general comes!

(ROMEO enters.)

ROMEO: Come, men of England! To battle let us wend.
(Addressing SOLDIER #2)
Thou—nameless soldier! You!
What call the locals yonder field, my friend?

SOLDIER #2: It's Bosworth.

ROMEO:
Then name we this the Battle of Bosworth Field!

ALL: Bosworth Field!

SOLDIER #2: No, my name's Bosworth.

WALES: Young Romeo, we praise thy courage, lord.

ROMEO:
I thank thee, Duke of Wales, who joins the fray,
And all stout English allies on this day.
O, let me grip thy forearm manfully.

WALES: I come attached with other noblemen:
The Duke of Kent, brave Northumberland,
And here the goodly Earl of Sandwich serves.

ROMEO: This day shall make thee hero, Sandwich.

SANDWICH: Thanks!
I think it meet. I'll proud be England's club!

(Enter the EARL OF ATHOL.*)*

ATHOL: Young Romeo, my forces have arrived!

ROMEO: The noble Earl of Athol!

ATHOL: Not so loud.

ROMEO: Thy name's proclaiméd loud on every road.

OTHERS: Aye, Athol! True, Athol!

ROMEO: Mighty Athol, what numbers take the field?

ATHOL: Every man I have, all bold and true.

WALES: And I the highland shrubs did beat with stick
To raise a posse up; they're here at hand.

ROMEO: O, Bless the day!

ATHOL: So, counting English, Welsh, and several Scot,
We've twenty-six.

ROMEO: And Rome?

ATHOL: We hear they've brought
Some twenty thousand.

SOLDIER #2: O, I just forgot;
I'm due at home. I'm wrapping up some gifts
To celebrate Saint Crispin's with the kids.

ROMEO: Then get thee home; the happier twenty-five
To honor England with the bleeding wounds
That we contract on this Saint Crispin's Day!
Who is this sainted Crispin, by the way?

WALES: The patron saint of shoe care professionals.†

ATHOL: Then rise we up, and like Saint Crispin go!
With polished pumps, and—let's—keep our tongues!
Lace up our courage like…like a shoe—
May our soles— Turn not our heels— Ah!
Pox on poesy! Damn the metaphor!
We're men of England! S'balls, let's go to war!
(He exits.)

ROMEO: Fly—you mighty Athol!‡

OTHERS: Aye, Athol! Go, Athol!

WALES: Good Romeo, the Welsh will lead the charge:
And yonder lies a basket full of leeks,
A native sprig of Wales we wear for luck!

ROMEO:
Then lead thee, Duke! And each man take a leek,
That we—we lucky few, might victory eke!
(Exuent.)

---

† *It's true*

‡ *In 3rd Quarto, ROMEO's line is punctuated "Fly you— mighty Athol!" Pollard prefers this reading as slightly less derogatory encouragement.*

Scene 3

(PHYCUS' *Castle*)

(*Alarum bells a-tolling. Enter* MACBETTY.)

MACBETTY: Let tartan banners deck th' outward walls;
Their thickly thread-count and our castle strong
Repel the Roman horde of its attack,
Or any English knight who'd filch it back!

(*Enter* GLOUCESTER)

GLOUCESTER: This falls out better than I could devise!
The Brits and Romans slaughter off themselves
Whilst we cheer forth from safety's citadel.
One trepidation frets me.

MACBETTY: What is wrong?

GLOUCESTER: I can't recall which side we're fighting on.

(*Enter* CLOWN *and* FRIAR.)

MACBETTY: What ho, what make you here?

CLOWN: Reviléd lord and lady, tis with dread
I must report...sweet Juliet is dead.

MACBETTY: The princess dead!

FRIAR: Quite dead. I felt her heart.
And gave her mouth to mouth, but twould not start.

GLOUCESTER: Alack! I did so want a wedding night.
Is she still warm?

FRIAR: Nay, m'lord. Cold.

GLOUCESTER: How cold?

MACBETTY: Go, Friar Don,
Speed her lifeless body to the grave,
And do her rites with all alacrity,
Ere necro-boy does some monstrosity.

FRIAR: But first I must this letter quick dispatch.
Tis full of grave import.

GLOUCESTER: She was not warm?
I find that strange. An autopsy perform
To glean the cause of Juliet's demise!

FRIAR: Methinks again. My letter here can wait.
Saints and angels, bless young Romeo's fate.
Should this my missive miss it's postage-date.
Come, Sirrah.

(*Exit* FRIAR *and* CLOWN.)

MACBETTY:
Then Richard, I rule alone—the law demands
Thou canst be king sans Juliet's wedding banns.

GLOUCESTER:
If I find Hamlet first, twill thwart thy plans.
(*Calling off*)
Fetch my armor! Saddle up my steed!
I sprint to war with all allowéd speed!

(GLOUCESTER *exits with some difficulty, as* CLOWN
reenters.)

CLOWN: M'Lady?

MACBETTY: Now what news?

CLOWN: A fresh report from off the field of war.

MACBETTY: Yes?

CLOWN: From out the castle window, even now
I saw... Methinkst I saw— Don't hold me to't...

MACBETTY: Spit it, Wheyface! Saw you what?

CLOWN: The trees of Birnam Wood march off their hill.
And that twould be 'bout it. I'd best get back.
(*He exits.*).

MACBETTY: The trees uproot and march; it cannot be.
My spell of fortune came with warrantee!
I'll to the battle; Bring armor, club and shield!

Holla, Gloucester. We head for Bosworth Field!
(*He exits.*)

Scene 4

(*A wilderness nowhere near the cliffs of Dover*)

(*Enter* PHYCUS *and* HAMLET. *The old king wears a wreath of flowers and under-knickers.*)

HAMLET: Good Nuncle, nay! Tis witless suicide
To be out flower-picking in thy shorts
When storms and battles brew! Caloo, callay!

PHYCUS: Leave me, Yorick! Jest to me no more!

HAMLET: I've a droll one and a merry, Nuncle-butt.

PHYCUS: Thy jokes yield neither lessons nor a laugh;
What, three-legg'd men at evening use a cane?

HAMLET: Hey, nonny!

PHYCUS: Take me, Fool, to Dover's high-flung cliff
That I may toss my weary self to death.

HAMLET: As Fortune would supply, we stand e'en now
Upon the lip of Dover's precipice.
Hark, hear the raging wind and sea below!

(HAMLET *breathes a steady whistling wind in* PHYCUS's *face.*)

PHYCUS:
I hear it! Blow thou wind, and chap my cheeks!
Smell the salt-sea air! Of fish it reeks!

PHYCUS: Fool, constrain me not; I long to leap.

HAMLET: But ere thou dost, confess of any crimes
Thy guilty, sinful conscience may contain.
Toward heaven, hell, or limbo leap thee clean;
First fess up, Father, how you killed thy queen!

PHYCUS: I killed her not! I wished it oft enough,
But ere I found the means or will to do't,
The vicious Tartan traitress beat me to't.

HAMLET: Macbetty!

PHYCUS: Yea! Why sound you so surprised?
Her husband was my son, a fruited cake
Much noted for his Oedipus-al crush;
And fearing she might lose her royal spot,
Macbetty murder'd Gertrude.

HAMLET: So that's the plot!

PHYCUS: And now my soul is scrubb'd of sin's decay,
I long to snuff it.

HAMLET: Nuncle, leap away!

PHYCUS: Geronimus!
(He takes a face-first dirt dive.)
Yorick, how'd I do?

HAMLET: (Calling as from a great height)
A miracle! You did not fall but flew.
Let Yorick aid thee, Nuncle, til anon
Like foolish moon, he'll prove thy rising son.

PHYCUS: Unhand me, Fool! Or catch me on the run!

HAMLET: Nuncle!

(Exuent PHYCUS and HAMLET, running.)

Scene 5

(Bosworth Field. A swelling battle montage.)

(BRUTUS enters opposite WALES and SOLDIER #2.)

BRUTUS: Come you English, bring your claymores on,
That I might have some steel to clank upon!

WALES: Turn, proud Brutus; steel thyself in vain
And be the first to fall in our campaign!

(PHYCUS *and* HAMLET *rush through the scene.*)

HAMLET:
Once more into thy breaches, Sire! Once more!

PHYCUS: Let the fiery youth of England look askance
To see the governing body without pants!

(*Exeunt* HAMLET *and* PHYCUS.)

WALES: Have at you, Brutus! Charge, young Bosworth,
go!

(BRUTUS *battles* SOLDIER #2 *and* WALES, *until their
engagement travels off stage.*)

(*Enter* MACBETTY *with a bag of golfing clubs.*)

MACBETTY:
"Fear not til Birnam Wood do up and march."
Said not the bitch-fiend? Aye! Now by report
Old Birnam up and marches off its slopes!
Well let it be. Come, clubs! Come wrack!
At least I'll die with irons on my back.

(*Enter* SANDWICH *and* EXTRANIUS, *fighting.*)

EXTRANIUS: At blow for blow I match thee on the field!

SANDWICH:
Thou art out-sported, Roman; drop and yield.

EXTRANIUS: I shant be ransomed; nay, at any price.

SANDWICH:
Then battle forth, and be by Sandwich sliced.

(SANDWICH *and* EXTRANIUS *fight and exit.*)

MACBETTY: I'll climb this lofty perch, to better view
What fortunes fall the victors of this war.

(*A series of shouts: first anxious, then jubilant.*)

(*Enter in* WALES, SOLDIER #2, *and* SANDWICH, *with*
BRUTUS *and* EXTRANIUS *bound.*)

WALES: Bless our victory, Heaven; the day is won!
The leather-skirted Romans turn and run,
And these two ransomed rascals wait their doom.
Suggesteth I we dress them up as clowns,
And run a spanking gauntlet in the square.

BRUTUS: Just kill me.

OTHERS: Nay!

MACBETTY: How won you victory being so outmann'd?

SOLDIER #2: The Welshman fought like Hercules!

WALES: Nay, Bosworth, thou;
Thou fought like Hercules! Thou's the man!

SOLDIER #2: Nay, thou's the man!

WALES: And Sandwich was a Manwich, making meal
Of every Roman rival!

SANDWICH: Thou dost forget,
Twas Romeo our glorious gambit plann'd:
We ran like chickens into Birnham Wood,
Pursued by Romans to the mountain's base;
He had us hew down every fir and pine,
Igniting them afire, and roll'd 'em down.
A man'uver worthy of ancient Spartecus!

WALES: Nay, thou art Spartecus!

SANDWICH: Thou art Spartecus! Thou!

MACBETTY: Then Birnham Wood is fell'd!

SOLDIER #2: Tis very true:
Every tree was lumber'd off or burnt.
For this shall Romeo doubtlessly be named
The Minister of Forest Management.

WALES: Go seek the gentleman!

(The Englishmen huddle happily.)

BRUTUS: They watch us not, Extranius; let us make
Like antique Romans and dispatch ourselves.
I have a blade within my waistband. Here!

EXTRANIUS:
My hands are pinioned; hold for me the knife.
When dead, I'll do the same and take thy life.
Jove, take my soul for Rome and liberty!

(EXTRANIUS *leaps upon* BRUTUS' *back, and moans loudly.*)

SANDWICH:
Zounds! I swear, you do but turn your back...

EXTRANIUS: I am dead!

(EXTRANIUS *slides from* BRUTUS' *back and falls into the wings.*)

BRUTUS: Without a sword or other earthly blade,
I die e'en now—of shear embarrassment.

(BRUTUS *slowly slides to the ground in a tragic "death by shame".*)

WALES: Bear these bodies off, some of you.

(SOLDIER #2 *exits, gently kicking* BRUTUS *off stage.*)

(ROMEO *enters.*)

ROMEO:
The day is ours; friend Wales, and Sandwich, too,
O let me grip thy forearms manfully.
The Romans count their bodies; lost there are
Some eighteen thousand soldiers, give or take.

SANDWICH: How many English?

ROMEO: One. The Duke of Bunt.
His memory we silently reflect.
Good—
Some of you go, spread news the day is ours.

SANDWICH & WALES:
And so we shall, and very willingly.
(*They exit.*)

ROMEO: Now tell, Macbetty, how is my new-wed wife?
How fares my lovely Juliet at home?

MACBETTY:
Thy wife is dead, enshrined in Phycus' tomb.
Poison is the cause, by her own hand.

ROMEO: You lie, Macbetty, curses on thy head.

MACBETTY: Go seek thyself her stone-slab bridal bed.
At Death's cold storehouse is she registréd.

(ROMEO *departs, followed by* MACBETTY.)

(GLOUCESTER *and a young* LAD *enter severally.*)

GLOUCESTER:
Why can't they fight their wars on level ground?
A horse! A horse! My kingdom for a horse!

LAD: Truly?

GLOUCESTER: Aye.

LAD: A deal! My family's horse is tied to yonder tree.

(GLOUCESTER *exits. The* LAD *remains alone.*)

LAD: When shall we expect the kingdom then?
Hello?
(*He exits.*)

Scene 6

(*A graveyard near Castle Phycus*)

(*Enter* HAMLET *as Yorick, and* PHYCUS, *blind.*)

HAMLET: We've made it seems a journey circular
And at the castle are we now returned.
The graveyard, now I see. What man is this?

(Enter a GRAVEDIGGER, *singing.)*

GRAVEDIGGER: She's dead and gone, dig up the lawn,
She must be buried beneath the berms.
Lay her beneath a posy wreath,
Where none of her lovers can see the worms!
The worms crawl in, the worms crawl out,
In her gullet and out her snout… Hie-dee-ho.
(He whistles happily.)

HAMLET: A jolly dirger. Sirrah, who's grave is this?

GRAVEDIGGER: Who's isn't it! I've not dug as deep as a frat boy's wit, but have disturbed the bones of two and twenty, give or take a leg. Merry, here's a skull.

HAMLET: Let me see't. Alas! Dost thou think, sirrah, all men come to this?

GRAVEDIGGER:
Aye, and women, too. Teen models, 'specially.

PHYCUS: Sirrah, if a king may die, and turn to loam; and loam be used to stop a barrel; might not Mighty Alexander e'en now plug a bunghole?

GRAVEDIGGER: M'lord, from what I've read, Alexander did indeed plug a bunghole every now and then.

*(*PHYCUS *takes the skull.)*

PHYCUS: Who's skull was this?

GRAVEDIGGER:
That were Yorick's skull, the king's jester.
(He exits.)

PHYCUS:
If Yorick's dead: then good-man, who art thou,
That for this week companions me with care,
Providing food and countless knock-knock jokes?

HAMLET: Look up, dear father. Hamlet, here your son.
Do but look up.

(PHYCUS *swings his tethered eye to espy* HAMLET.)

PHYCUS: My son, forgiveth me!

HAMLET: (*Being hit by tear drops*)
Father, do not weep.

(FRIAR *enters.*)

FRIAR: Prince Hamlet, I have found you; and the king!
The war is won, but danger stalks you still.
Into the castle quick, before— alas, too late!

(*Enter* MACBETTY *and* GLOUCESTER.)

MACBETTY: Phycus, turn thee now! Thy in-laws call,
To do the deed neglected long ago:
Tis time to die!

GLOUCESTER: This blade shall make it so;
For double dastardy, my foil's point
With Friar's poison here I do anoint.

MACBETTY:
Come thou villain, blind and scantly dressed;
Be slain by us!

PHYCUS: I willing ope my breast!

HAMLET: Tyrants, stay! Thou shall not harm his grace!

GLOUCESTER:
Have at thee, slave; and perish in his place!

(GLOUCESTER *with sword and* HAMLET *with* PHYCUS's
walking staff do fight. HAMLET *is hit.*)

FRIAR: Hamlet, thou art hit!

HAMLET: Tis but a scratch.

GLOUCESTER: A nick enough the poison to dispatch!

HAMLET: Behold, my mother's ghost!

(*As* GLOUCESTER *looks away,* HAMLET *disarms him.*)

HAMLET: Ha! Made you look!

GLOUCESTER: Disarméd by the oldest trick in book!

HAMLET: And with a trick, I trump thee!

(HAMLET *wounds* GLOUCESTER.)

GLOUCESTER: I'm a schnook!
Who art thou, knave, that sends me to the grave?

HAMLET: I Hamlet am.

GLOUCESTER: But you're of woman born.
The damnéd witch mistook my destiny!
Hamlet, ere we fade, I'll disclose all:
Twas thine own wife, Macbetty, killed the queen!

MACBETTY:
I ne'er did love you, wimpling, but to scheme.

HAMLET: Too wimply for revenge. Absolve me, Friar!

(FRIAR *massages* HAMLET's *shoulders*.)

FRIAR:
Good night, Sweet Prince! And nap thee for a spell;
The unction in thy wound was poison free,
But rather some of Juliet's sleeping draught!
Now go to sleep.

HAMLET: To sleep?

FRIAR: Perchance to dream.

HAMLET: Ah, there's the rub.

(HAMLET *and* GLOUCESTER *fall.*)

PHYCUS: My son is dead! Compounding my regret
I never made amends with Juliet!

FRIAR: Then get thee to the chapel monument—

PHYCUS: My daughter's there? My sweeting!

(PHYCUS *exits, as* FRIAR DON *attempts to follow.*)

FRIAR: Don't look yet!

MACBETTY: Friar, hold thy peace! If I be doom'd,
I shall be-doom you all!

FRIAR: Beshrew thy villainy;
One speech I'll make and all ends happily!

MACBETTY:
Churlish monks should vows of silence make;
Then silent be, while out thy tongue I take!

FRIAR: But they'll think Juliet is dead!

(MACBETTY *removes* FRIAR's *tongue.*)

(PHYCUS *enters with "dead"* JULIET.)

PHYCUS: Never, never, never, never, never...
Never, never... Wilt someone help me here!
I'm blind and old!

(MACBETTY *helps place* JULIET *on a tomb.*)

PHYCUS: Juliet, cold and dead! I must be mad;
Methinks I see her stomach rise and fall.
And there again! Does no one else behold it?

(FRIAR *gestures wildly.*)

PHYCUS: What, spastic monastic? Do not interfere;
This scene of tragic death—

(HAMLET *and* GLOUCESTER *rise with a gasp.*)

PHYCUS: 'Ods zombies!

MACBETTY: See you that!
They stay not dead; like dogs and democrats!
Art flesh or spirit?

HAMLET: No apparition known
Need spur my hot revenge! You vile crone!

(HAMLET *with blade, and* MACBETTY *with golfing club,*
battle. Eventually, HAMLET *disarms her.*)

HAMLET: Take this club, you foul infectious hag!
The course now played, I'll stick it in the bag!

(HAMLET *drives the club down* MACBETTY's *throat. She dies.*)

GLOUCESTER: Join her, prince! My villainy awakes!

(GLOUCESTER *stabs* HAMLET, *who falls into the wings.*)

HAMLET: I am dead! Alas, young Romeo comes!
(As ROMEO*)*
My brother Hamlet? Zounds, thou hast been hurt!
(As HAMLET*)*
Go not unto the graveside, Romeo!
(As ROMEO*)*
Let go me, Hamlet.
(As HAMLET*)*
Nay, go not in. Ill fortune governs here!

PHYCUS:
My children both are dead. My old heart breaks.
Look, look! A wisp of breath upon her lips.
(Dangling his eye over her face)
She lives. Do you see? Do you see?

(PHYCUS *dies.* ROMEO *enters.*)

ROMEO: Where is the king? The bitter wars are won.
But now I fear my Juliet's undone.

GLOUCESTER:
The king is dead, and there your lifeless bride.
Victims both of intrigue's homicide.

ROMEO: Gloucester, I am for you! This kindly king
Became my father when Juliet took my ring!

GLOUCESTER:
E'en now, e'en here, I was from death restorn!
I can't be killed by man of woman born.

ROMEO: Then Gloucester know thy fate: since I was ten
I've worked in politics as Caesar's friend;
My party membership I did not end:
Thus, I am—a card-carrying Caesarian!

GLOUCESTER:
A mighty reach—of Fate; but if cursed by thee,
Lay on, say I! And food for worms I'll be!
(GLOUCESTER and ROMEO fight. GLOUCESTER is killed, and falls into the wings.)

ROMEO: Someone call the Earl of Athol.

GLOUCESTER: *(Off)* O, I am slain!

ROMEO: And I with Juliet shall here remain!
Dear love, I will be faithful to my pact,
And drink to thee;
(To FRIAR)
How long til it react?
Thus with a kiss I die!
(Kiss)
Thus with a kiss I—
(JULIET sits up)

JULIET: Hie!

(ROMEO dies. ATHOL arrives.)

ATHOL: Juliet, come! Forsake this sepulcher.

JULIET: Gentle Athol! Where's my Romeo?
Why lie they all about? Tis like the family room,
When Christmas feasting's done, and all do swoon.
What! my father dead? And Romeo, poisonéd!
Perchance there's toxic traces on his tongue—ah, no!
And in this vile, no tragic backwash left!
Then here I take this happy weapon up,
Pierce my navel, and let me die!
(She stabs herself and dies).

ATHOL: Can any here explain what mishaps fell,
To load this hallowed lawn so heavily?
What man can speak?

(FRIAR steps forward.)

FRIAR: Mffffl, rffffffl, bfffffl, kfffffl, flllllfffff,
Rfffffffl, nffffffffl, mffffffffl, etc.

ATHOL: We thank thee, Friar, for thy woeful tale.
In time, we trust, you'll have it written down.
A glooming peace this evening with it brings,
The sun for sorrow, hides behind a cloud;
Go hence, and tell thy neighbors of these things;
Next time we do't, perhaps we'll draw a crowd.
For never was there play of such pedigree,
As this of Phycus, and his family.
(A beat.)
I'm talking to myself.
Go, bid the gravediggers scoop!

(Drums and trumpets, then curtain.)

(The players rise, bow, and dance a lively bergomask.)

END OF PLAY

FINALE TUNE

(Sung to a tune suggestive of When That I Was and a Little Tiny Boy.*)*

(Inclusion optional)

(Building a harmonic chord)

When that I wert
When that I wert
When that I wert
When that I wert...

When that I wert but a player on the stage,
With a Hey, Ho, to be rememberéd,
I'd act my deaths with a melancholy rage
For the Critics only love you when you're good and
    dead.

When that the script wert a scribble on the page,
With a Hey, Ho, to be rememberéd,
It's death-count topped the Elizabethan Age
For the Critics only love you when you're good and
    dead.

Now with our crowd it is time to disengage,
With a Hey, Ho, to be remembered,
The Bard of Stratford told it like a sage
How the Critics only love you when you're good
How the Critics only love you when you're good

How the Critics only love you when you're good...
    and dead.

www.ingramcontent.com/pod-product-compliance
Lightning Source LLC
Chambersburg PA
CBHW052205090426
42741CB00010B/2420